Christmas Glory

Advent Readings to Draw You into Wonder

Pierce Taylor Hibbs

Contents

I

The Passion in a Promise

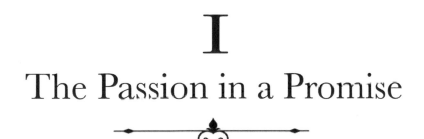

We easily forget what goes into a promise: the future. Promises stare into the beyond and say, "Yes. I will go there." They travel into the dark out of love, out of passion, out of unexplainable joy. And they wait there, in the silence. They wait for the present. The present will have no idea what's coming, of course. The present will get blindsided. And that's a good thing. That's a Christmas thing.

All the way back in Genesis 3:9, there was a promise that came unspoken. In the dim light of ancestral history, Adam and Eve were told clearly what would happen to them if they disobeyed. Then they disobeyed, but death *didn't* come, did it? It was just the quiet, the sound of their own feet swishing through the grass and planting their bodies behind a bush. The promise came in a question: *where are you?*

That doesn't sound like much of a promise, does it? But it is. The question opened a door for them to a different future. What they thought was the future for them, given their decision to disobey, was death. But the question directed them to another future—a warm hearth of fellowship with a God who already knew where they were are, where they'd been, and where they would be. For the God who knows *all*, the question *where are you?* is brimming with meaning. And chief among those meanings is the divine decision to show grace. God says, in effect, "I know where you are, but do *you*? Even though you've gone away, I see you. And I'm showing grace. I'm going to help you find yourself, find your way back to me."

Who knew that the salvation of the world, the divine answer to all things broken and bleak, would start with a question? *Where are you?*

And think of the answer, that promise resting in the future, silent and serene like an infant. Yes, now it makes beautiful sense that the answer to all our buried hope would be a baby, God in the flesh. What else could wait so perfectly for us? What else could blindside the present but God as a child? How, with a wild wonder, could the present have ever imagined *this*? This was God's answer to that ancient question. *Where are you?* God would answer in the future. "Right here. And I'm with you. Hold me in your hands if you like. One day soon, *my* hands will hold *you*, even as they're stretched out and pinned to the wood I spoke into being."

Christmas is the joy of promise. It is the day of the great answer—the answer to the question that God himself asked at the beginning. *Where are you?* Right here. Right here, with you.

2
What Eyes Can See

My eyes are getting worse. I remember it every year when I look at our Christmas tree, gleaming gold with little amber stars, singing its quiet anthem into the dark of the room. I stare at the tree every year without my glasses on as a reminder that the world is blurring with time. My eyes see *less*. Every line of light is melting. I imagine what it will be like one day to be blind, to see only shadows, to dream of color in knife-sharp contours, to take in not just more light but more definition.

This all may sound depressing for Advent season, but I write with a smile on my face. We're all fading floral. Some of us have enough color in our petals and vigor in our stem to pretend that death is a dream. Others of us are more aware of mortality. But the truth is truth for all of us. And what I stare at in my mind's eye each Christmas is what lies behind the blindness, something my eyes can't currently see. But my heart can see it, clear as a Pennsylvania hillside on a cold December morning.

What is it? It's hard to describe. Imagine a golden afternoon, where warm light is pouring in through the windows, and you're sitting contentedly on a couch, strangely aware that this particular afternoon will *never* end. You will be able to talk casually with God himself, holed up in your living room with an old afghan on his lap. Friends and family enter the room and raise their cheeks, showing their teeth in silence. The quiet, unending community . . . *that* is what my heart sees. Christmas is a memorial for warm-blooded, unending *communion*.

I wonder what you see this year, from your living room. There's a way to look *through* the room, to take off your glasses and let the lines blur.

You will see *more* in a sense, not *less*.

The old shepherds, gathering around the rough-hewn timber of a commoner's manger on that starry night, likely didn't see everything with 20-15 vision. Eyeglasses, after all, didn't appear on the pages of human history until thirteenth century Italy, donning the noses of quiet monks. These shepherds surely saw light, though the lines and textures of what they saw may have been blurred a bit. But that was not the point of the evening.

They beheld in that little stable a *person* who was light beyond light, the light behind all lights. That infant light didn't burn like the fiery sun, fierce and blinding, assaulting their retinas. No . . . it burned quiet, long, and slow, bright enough for them to know that something was different. Something had changed. The infant drew their souls in like moths. It captivated with its quiet; it beckoned with its shallow breaths, soft and simple, like the raising and lowering of a monarch's wings at the end of migration.

And it *was* a migration. God had come south to stay, down from the unsearchable northern Alps of divinity. He had come from a place so far above us that not even a craning neck stood a chance of perceiving it on the horizon. God had come in his tribe of three: Son from Father by Spirit. He had come at the end of an evening, but he had come to *make* evening unending. He had come to cast communion down on us like starlight.

This is what I think of each year when I stare, bleary-eyed, at our Christmas tree, gazing at the green and gold without my glasses on. So what if the lines are blurred and the colors are melting together? The real beauty is behind all that. The real beauty is the unending afternoon of fellowship with God and his great afghan. The real beauty is what eyes cannot see. Except you *can* see it, if you pull your glasses off, maybe even shut your eyes, and let your heart stare at the warm hope of communion. Christmas is a time for staring.

3

A Deeper Magic

E vil hardly ever works out the way we think it will. Evil enters the labyrinth of God's providence like a blind man, feeling his way around the high cinder-block walls and unexpected turns. It exits when God wills, after it's already served his purposes. But we don't often see evil this way, or even believe in God's providence. We think of evil as a sharp shooter with lethal precision and unchecked freedom. Christmas is a reminder that evil, when it comes to it, can't even stand up to an infant.

In C. S. Lewis's *The Lion, the Witch, and the Wardrobe*, Lucy mourns the death of her great lion, Aslan. Stabbed to the heart on a stone slab, surrounded by evil minions, Aslan appears lost. But then a *deeper magic* set in place by the Emperor beyond the Sea snapped that evil reality in half like a twig. Aslan rose from the dead. What appeared to be done was undone; an alleged victory for evil became its own death toll. C. S. Lewis knew it: evil exits the labyrinth of providence when God wills. In the end, no matter how horrid and horrendous it is, evil ends up being a servant, not a master.

Think of all this in the context of the Son of God breaking through a virgin's body to meet the light and air of our world, greeted by a chorus of grunts and foot-stomps from wet-nosed stable animals. Evil had been looking for the child, even before he was born. And evil would look for him after he entered the world (Matt. 2:16–18). But on the night of his birth, evil would not win (it never *really* does). The God of all things would enter the world he spoke, through the Word he spoke (John 1:1), by the Spirit who spoke it. Divine speech can't be silenced.

There is always a *deeper magic* at work around us. Evil seems to run rampant, to shred and break and burn without resistance. It rears its ugly head in global pandemics and mudslides, but also in a billion hateful words uttered by hearts deceived. In every case, it appears to stand over the situation, jamming its conqueror's flag into the soil of the moment, claiming clear victory—as the wicked witch did over Aslan's body. But evil is ignorant. It has no idea what God is up to. It boasts of desolation and a deep history of success, but something deeper undoes it.

That's Christmas. Christmas is the deeper magic of God burning bright as a star right in Satan's eyes. What was the evil it undid? Brace yourself . . . *our ignorant and selfish rebellion.* From the dawn of time, we have chosen *self* over *others, power* over *grace, revenge* over *forgiveness, taking* over *giving.* We've had a deep-seated desire to serve ourselves. But a deeper magic—the self-giving Trinity, maker and master of all things, who gave himself for us—would be born into our world and take over time: past, present, and future.

Christmas is the celebration of a deeper magic. It's a time to rejoice in truth that soars far above our heads. It's a time to smile uncontrollably at the unexpected providence of God. In the chess match for control over the hearts of men, Satan boasted of his every move. Then God showed up as a fleshy ball of dough, bleary-eyed, weak, and needy. Check mate. The deeper magic wins as Satan stares slack-jawed. Eternity saves time through an infant. What else can you do with that but raise your hands and say, "Hallelujah"?

4

Appearing in the Dark

I t isn't a coincidence that Christ was born
at night. Not all light comes through our
corneas. There is another kind of light, a
light of . . . *hope*. Christ in us is called "the
hope of glory" (Col. 1:27). And Christ is also the
light that shines in the darkness (John 1:5). Hope
shines. And what better time for a light to shine
than at night?

It's a hard concept to grasp, isn't it—that
a person can be a light? Maybe that's because it
isn't meant to be grasped; it's meant to be grown.
Some truths are hard and thick as granite. They
bear us up and keep us steady. But other truths are

seeds. They're meant to germinate, to stretch into a stem and lift their flowering head to the sun. This truth is like that. Christ as the light is Christmas greenery.

Imagine it. The night is dark and cold, air creeping in the folds of clothing as Joseph and Mary made their way to a small town. Caesar's decree for a census has swelled the town to its seams. Houses and inns are brimming. Streets are flooded with feet. Somehow, somewhere, Joseph and Mary find a stable. And there, amidst the heavy exhalations of cows and horses, amidst the pressing of hay under hooves, it would happen. In great pain, a light would dawn. But who would be able to see it?

Eventually, the whole world would see it, as the centuries rolled forward like boulders down a hill. People would stare at the story of Christ's birth and realize something more was happening than an infant pushing his head into a world of color and light. There was something . . . deeper.

Christmas is about the deeper light that takes focus to notice. And that deeper light is the God who gives himself away. Christ is, as the Nicene

Creed puts it, "Light of light, very God of very God." And why did he come? "For God so loved the world . . ." The *love* of God—even for those who ignore him or curse his name—culminates in *giving*. And that gift is "Light of light."

Follow me into this mystery. The light of the birth of Christ shines in gracious generosity; it glows because it gives. It sends a message to the whole world—chasing its own desires like a crazed dragonfly in the summer heat—that *others* are worth living for. Others are even worth *dying* for. But the Christ of Christmas shines brightest in the wonderful truth that other people are worth *God being born for*. How? Why? Because God made us like himself. We are his children.

If we take nothing else from the Christmas story, we take this: our world is darkened by selfishness. No light can come from those who stare at themselves. The darkness of that night so many years ago was a shadow of a deeper darkness. The light of God entered the world as self-giving grace. In that infant, God's hands were opened wide for any and all who wanted to grasp them. Jesus Christ is an invitation to live a life too great for selfishness, a life that seeks to give itself away for others. And the more we give, the brighter Christ burns in us.

This is why I've always loved singing "Silent Night" in a dark church, with all these hands holding amber candles. As we hold the light in our hands, together, we sing. And we sing not just *in* the dark but *through* the dark, out into the world that so desperately needs to have its chin lifted up, to have its focus taken off of itself, even for one day of the year.

Do you see? The Son of God was born on a dark night to give the light of self-giving to a selfish world. We stare at that infant each year and say, "Ah, yes, God. It's not about *me*." The light of God burns steadily through every season of our selfishness. But in this season, we pause intentionally to worship. The hope of God shines brightest in the darkest room. Creation, it turns out, is a room darker than any other. It needed a light. And the candle of God was lit on Christmas night.

5

The Donkey

Animals are a wonder because of their silence. They stand on the cusp of language, uttering with their eyes, whispering with their glances, beckoning with bending necks, fearing with folded ears. They have a wordless tongue. And in a strange sense, that's why we love them. Sincerity's home is silence.

And the donkey certainly seems sincere, doesn't it? A lowly beast to carry a lowly savior, a wordless worker to carry the Word for the world . . . The popular children's book *The Small One* portrays the donkey as a humble, self-sacrificing friend to a little boy. Towards the end of the book, when it looks as if the donkey will have to give his life up to help the boy, a kind stranger (Joseph) offers to buy him. The story ends with Small One carrying Mary into the blue moonlight to Bethlehem, bearing her on his little back without a grumble. Sounds like sincerity to me.

In reality, we only know one thing about that donkey: he didn't speak. With his head nodding to his own shifting steps, he carried on in quiet. He bore the mother who bore the savior who bore the sins of the world. It seems fitting that a wordless animal would usher in the most beautiful Word the world would ever hear. It's as if the donkey's life were the great pause before the voice of God broke through Mary's womb beneath a burning star. Silence is the arena for speech; the donkey was the arena for the Word of God. On that long trek to Bethlehem, under the navy sky, silence carried speech.

Christmas is hardly ever a time we associate with silence. Silver bells and Christmas carols, sure. But silence? And yet Christmas came on the back of silence, on the rough-haired hide of a donkey that would serve in secret. Christmas came to creatures who had trouble closing their mouths. The great irony is that the child of Christmas would eventually be described as a silent sheep who would not open his mouth (Isa. 53:7).

Why? Why would the Word for the world, who entered a silent night on a silent beast, not open his mouth when spoken against? Why not utter the truth, and perhaps even save himself through that? Why be like the donkey when he was more like the angel chorus of light, singing sweet salvation into the somber cities of men?

Maybe it was because, even all the way back on that first night of his life in the world, silence would still serve its purpose. It would still be the arena for speech, the pause before the utterance. And if that's how Christ came into the world, doesn't it make poetic sense for this echo at his exit? The pause, the silence, worn so well by a tired donkey, would come before the speech of resurrection. Jesus would go silent as a lamb before its shearers because the greatest thing he would even speak required a full breath, a full, back-from-the-depths-of-hell, born-of-water-and-the-Spirit, serpent-head-crushing breath.

When you sing "Silent Night" this year, think of the donkey. He doesn't get much credit for his silence, just as Christ doesn't get much credit for not opening his mouth before a delirious mob. But silence makes way for great speech. The dark makes way for the light. The donkey makes way for a King, the mute makes way for the majestic. I am thankful for the silent donkey that gave Christ the pause he needed before God spoke the most potent Word in all of history. *That*, my friends, is why that silent night is a *holy* night.

6

The Light Climbs Ever Higher

I have always been fascinated by the way our world grows outward and upward towards the light. The pine and maple trees in our yard stretch their trunks towards the sun because they're nourished by it. They *need* it. They are born in a black world of soil and rock, but not long after germination comes the blinding revelation of the sun. The light, it seems, is like a song that's growing fainter to them, and the only way to keep hearing it is to climb into the sky. The light calls upward. And if God is the light beyond all lights, the Light above our light, then it makes sense for so much upward light to be in focus for the Christmas story.

Start with the star. Take three foreign magi from the other side of the world. Set them on camels. Call them out into the dark with heads tilted toward the sky. A burning orb of white light flickers for their attention. And so they travel. They walk towards the light. They follow a holy call of luminosity. And that's fitting, since the infant will soon be called "the light of the world" (John 8:12). The magi are walking towards a light, marking the place where a greater light will emerge. Christmas is about chasing light.

What really draws me into awe is the casual statement that this burning orb in the sky *belongs* to someone. When the magi arrive at Herod's palace, they say, "Where is he who has been born king of the Jews? For we saw *his star* when it rose and have come to worship him" (Matt. 2:2). *His* star? An orb of hydrogen and helium was set burning in the black millions of miles away from our spinning planet on *his* account? What sort of God is this, who lights things on fire to announce his Son's coming?

And the star wasn't the only thing craning

our necks upward on that night. There was also a bright congregation of heavenly beings, singing not to a throng of spectators but to a handful of lowly shepherds.

And in the same region there were shepherds out in the field, keeping watch over their flock by night. And an angel of the Lord appeared to them, and the glory of the Lord shone around them, and they were filled with great fear. And the angel said to them, "Fear not, for behold, I bring you good news of great joy that will be for all the people. For unto you is born this day in the city of David a Savior, who is Christ the Lord. And this will be a sign for you: you will find a baby wrapped in swaddling cloths and lying in a manger." And suddenly there was with the angel a multitude of the heavenly host praising God and saying, "Glory to God in the highest, and on earth peace among those with whom he is pleased!" Luke 2:8–14

The glory of the Lord shone around them . .

. what must that light have been like? And yet, like the star's light, the aura of the angels was pointing beyond itself, not just to the God who made light but to the God who *is* light—the God who lights his own way.

All the lights of the Christmas story point beyond themselves. The light climbs ever higher, beyond even the highest rung of Jacob's ladder. What makes all of this so beautifully strange is that this God, who burned a star for his beloved and sent an angel chorus of light to sleepy shepherds, *this* God, Light beyond all light, came to the dark room of creation as an infant. Immeasurable Light came in a measured frame. The brightness of God could now touch and kick and speak. All the lights of the Christmas story—and all the twinkling lights hugging lamp posts and pine limbs at this time of year—call us to climb higher with our eyes. The God of light is here, in our dark world. He's *here*. The unimaginable Light came for *us*.

7

Longing for Snow

It's a childish thing, I know. But come late October, I can't help longing for snow. I don't why it excites me so much. Maybe I never really grew up. There's this scent heavy in the air, right before it starts to snow—a deep, weighted rawness, as if the sky has just shed it's invisible skin, and we're breathing in the fresh exterior. And then the flakes drift down, like some kind of carefree stardust. That sound of tiny footprints on the grass and pavement as the flakes meet the earth . . .

Snow hushes the world's harshness. It softens every corner, pads every surface, and rounds every edge. Everything hard, sharp, and rigid receives a white, whispered consolation. "It's alright," snow says. "Take it easy for a bit."

What has snow to do with Christmas? In a sense, maybe nothing. But I can't help but link snow with grace. I can't help but think of that tiny infant as a glorious lone snowflake settling on the earth, telling the whole world with his presence, "It's alright. Take it easy for a bit. I'm here." Rounding every edge of sin and suffering with his sympathy (Heb. 4:15), blanketing the pain and shards of shattered hope with consolation, covering *everything*—this is what Christ does. And he fell to us from heaven with all the fragility and Spirit-drifting whimsy of a thin ice sheet. Just think of the contrast between the thing and its surroundings: *ice crystals* falling through *an atmosphere* that can take them wherever it wills, tearing them in half or clumping them together; *the Son of God* arriving in the Spirit as a doughy infant with soft bones in *a world* that hated God. Why take the risk? I can only stare slack-jawed.

For God, on some mysterious continent of love in eternity, the risk was worth it. (And he had full control anyway, though we habitually disbelieve this.) He sent the Son out of *love*, not out of compulsion. The Son came voluntarily (for there's only one will in God), drifting down from the dark clouds of our own confusion, settling on *us*. We did as little to bring Christ down as we do to bring snow from the sky. It's all grace. All of it.

Maybe that, in the end, is why I always long for snow. I long for grace, for the free, unexpected, unanticipated, unimaginable gifts of a God who loves so fiercely that he doesn't just offer us presents; he offers us *persons*. He offers us himself. Isn't that cause enough to clap your hands at the winter window and scream out, "It's snowing!" My God, every time I hear a child shout that sentence, I think of the Christmas Gospel.

Longing for snow isn't so distant from longing for a savior, in the end. Both fall from heaven with a wild ecstasy and land on our shoulders. But only one of them can take us back up into the sky window of wonder.

8

All the Red and Green

Red and green evoke some visceral recognition of Christmas. Some people claim the colors as distinctly Christian—red for the blood of Christ and green for the evergreen of eternal life he gives. Others point to a 1930s Coca-Cola ad with a red-clad Santa and green fur tree. It's probably both, rich as the West is in its Christian history and poor as it is in its vain consumerism. In either case, it does get you thinking: *why do colors have meaning?*

With words, meaning seems less mysterious (though it isn't, upon closer examination). A series of letters corresponds to a concept or object in reality. That's enough to satisfy our superficial curiosity (though the truth about meaning in language runs far deeper). But with colors, things seem more subjective. That a wavelength of light could *mean* something . . . how did we get there?

One of the keys is that meaning lies in *memory*, the greatest asset of any human being. Memory is the treasure buried beneath our daily tasks, packages of time wrapped in ether, our little histories handed to us from God knows where. And color seems especially potent in conjuring up our memories, doesn't it?

All the red and green I start to see this time of year brings me right into a realm of unexplainable magic, where I walk roads of memory to transcend time. In an instant, I can be six years old again. The swirls of crimson on a candy cane, and how they faded into the white as I drew off the color with my tongue; the green gel of spearmint leaf candies, resting under a shell of shimmering sugar; the red yarn on my old stocking, covered with pulls and tabs from years of use; the green needles on our family fur tree, always ready to prick our eager fingers; the red hymnals we used in church to sing the first Christmas carols; the hunter green jacket of a nutcracker carrying tiny black fish. The colors call me. You have your own colors calling you, no doubt.

Still, *why do colors have meaning in our memory?* They have meaning because God controls the details of our days in *patterns*; in our waking seconds, filled with reds and greens, God is there, busy in his incessant patterning with particulars, with the things that strike our nostrils or bump into our finger tips. "Look at this. Touch that. Taste this. Listen in." Over time, our memory swells, and then we see the patterns. They're not all binary, a series of ones and twos. They're more complicated, more textured, more varied and intricate. We can't even fully identify them with any precision. But we know them. We recognize them like old friends. Our patterns live in our memories, but it is God who controls the patterns, who lines up our experiences and calls us to interpret them in himself (Acts 17:28).

Wherever you are right now, pause. Gather your patterns of red and green. Praise God for the power and pain of memory, for the searing reds and settled greens. The colors call us, we think, into our halls of memory. But listen more closely to them. It is *God* who is calling. Through our halls of memory, his voice is calling us to patterns he has given, but beneath all the patterns is a divine *person*, who took on the patterns of man in order to show us the patterns of God. I can't tell you all the things that live in those divine patterns. But I do know of something called *grace*, which ran red with blood one day and now is evergreen.

9

Breathe in the Cold

One of my favorite pastimes each Christmas season is to go outside to take in a long, deep breath, and then let it out slowly. I count in sets of five: five seconds in, five seconds hold, five seconds out. This sends a surge of oxygen into my eyes, slows my heartbeat, and releases a cloud of vapor into the icy air. The vapor is the result of moisture condensing into tiny drops of water as my warm breath meets the cold air. The clash of temperatures creates a mist. And then the mist disappears. "What is your life? For you are a mist that appears for a little time and then vanishes" (James 4:14). My whole life is like that one momentary breath in the cold.

Something similar happened, I think, when Jesus Christ was born. The fiery holiness of God met the openly cold world that night. The heat of holiness met the cold of a calloused humanity. Was there a vapor? The vapor was his life of love. It hung in the air for just over thirty years before vanishing, like us.

But it was different. The vapor of his life didn't vanish; it ascended. It went to be with others—with his Father and the Spirit, the ancient family. And the vapor is still there, immune to the disease of *ending*. The vapor ever lives to make intercession for our vapors (Rom. 8:34).

But there's something more . . . a Christmas gift we never saw coming. It's true that Christ ascended, and yet he came to give *us* his life, not to take it with him somewhere else. "I came that they may have life and have it abundantly" (John 10:10). Abundant life, *his* life, a life born and empowered by the very Spirit of God. This is what we have? Do you believe that? Do I?

The wonder of Christmas mirrors the mystery of that vanishing vapor I watch flow from my lips each winter. Christ came not to give us encouragement or hope or comfort (though he did give us all of those things, too). He came to give us *himself*. He came that we might have life, but *he* is the life (John 14:6). He is the resurrection (John 11:25). He is the vapor that never really vanishes. And when he came into the world on that Christmas night, *his* night, that was the warm breath of God for a winter world.

I continue my tradition. It's cold enough now for me to see my breath. The time is ripe, like a mid-October apple. I breathe in the cold and let out the vapor. And now when I do this, I think of baby Jesus, my vapor, my life, and how he met me two thousand years ago, met my cold world (still shivering in its stubbornness), became the vapor that I would take in by faith, so many years later. *My* life is *his* mist now. I'm never really going to vanish. The grace of God's giving has made me a lasting mist in Christ. Hallelujah.

10

Carols in the Night

———◆———

Every year, the little church of my childhood, shepherded by my father, would go Christmas caroling. I don't see this so much anymore, and it makes me sad. There's something to be missed in having strangers randomly show up at your door in the night, boldly offering sound as a gift in the dark. It's the epitome of grace, isn't it? Something good and beautiful just shows up unannounced, unanticipated.

I don't remember any of the faces of those whom we sang to over the years. The awkward tension, eased only by the voices that found themselves partway through an initial stanza, took more of my attention. But I remember this feeling, when each person opened the door and leaned into the light, half-smiling and half-amazed. And for just a few minutes, a pathway of eyes locked in. They stared at us, and we stared at them—everything else in the whole world falling away. There was a deep satisfaction in being a part of something that went well beyond me.

Those memories of caroling at night are like jewels in the crown of my Christmas remembrance. Whenever I think of them, I wonder. I wonder if something like Christmas carol grace was there that night, when Christ was born. Despite all the calls of the prophets, the ancient words pointing to the coming Messiah, no one knew exactly when he would come, save three magi marveling at a star in the east. Christ came unanticipated, during the night, the most beautiful Word of God uttered when we weren't expecting it. He showed up on the doorstep of humanity surrounded by stable animals. And there was that staring, too—the sounds of Bethlehem fading into the background as Joseph and Mary realized that they were a part of something much bigger than themselves, something God-sized, a Christmas carol sung directly to them by God himself. What could they do in that moment besides stare and smile?

Christ is our Christmas carol. He showed up on that first Christmas night, wholly good and beautiful, unanticipated. He was born of the Spirit, sent by the Father, a triune gift we could open again and again and again. This is the season for staring, the season for joyful recognition that we are a small part of something much greater, a song that God is singing as we stand on the doorstep of the present.

II

Looking for Lights

W e did it at least once every year. We went looking for lights. My three brothers and I would pack into the minivan, stuffing our puffy winter coats underneath the seat-belts. With mom and dad at the helm, we'd turn out of our driveway into a world of darkness, hoping to find something worthy of awe. Each of us began staring out the side windows, searching for Christmas lights that went truly above and beyond.

There were the usuals: little Santa sleighs pulled by reindeer—six for the cheaper displays, eight for the more expensive ones; giant Frosty the Snowman, glowing white and happily bloated; rainbow lights weaving their ways around walkway shrubs; and a series of manger displays, some gaudy and cartoonish and others simple and serious. Every house was trying to speak through its Christmas light display, even the ones that lacked Christmas lights.

My favorite ones were the pure, white-light displays, where every tree and shrub was wrapped in glowing jewels, matched by strands of lights on the gutters. The serious houses did their shrub wrapping meticulously so that the shape of the shrub stood as a perfect silhouette behind the lights. Those were the ones that always caught my eyes. I didn't know why back then, but I think it's because I loved the way the lights dressed the shrubs and trees like coats on standing bodies. On some displays, the lights seemed to be jerked into place, as if the people were putting straight jackets on the greenery. But with these it was different. Someone had carefully dressed the bushes and small fur trees, taking care of the plants' comfort, in a sense.

We continued the tradition with our kids. And there's one house—a mansion that looks more like a hotel than a house—with a host of carefully dressed trees. But these trees—they're giant, some sixty feet tall, and several thirty or forty feet. And *every* one of them is wrapped in lights to the very tip. I have no idea how they do it, but it must be professional. It's breath-taking, like a whole city of lights, with real skyscrapers to boot. I feel like a kid staring at a toy factory as we drive by. Every year I tell my wife I just want to run down the long driveway screaming "Joy to the World." She reminds me every year that this would be trespassing and that I wouldn't dare. Every year I smile a what-if smile. A city of lights with real golden skyscrapers . . .

That's all very different from the world little Jesus entered two thousand years ago, a place where the navy night was lit only by distant stars and the torches or lanterns of those who *needed* the light for something. And yet, there were still some who went searching for the lights. Well, there were three who went searching for *a* light, for a star. "When they saw the star, they rejoiced exceedingly with great joy. And going into the house, they saw the child with Mary his mother, and they fell down and worshiped him" (Matt. 2:10–11).

Joy and *worship*—that's what they had upon witnessing the first Christmas light display, where the light was a *person* wrapped not in twinkling amber but in blankets. And still, he shone brilliantly enough to demand joy, worship, and gifts.

We're always looking for lights. But we can never forget what made that first Christmas night spectacular. That one, humble Christmas in the two-thousand-year-old dark is our constant reminder that the light of the world came looking for *us*. He came knowing that he wouldn't be noticed by many, but those who would notice him, those who would stare at his face as if it were a life-giving star of God, would remember not what they found but how they *were found*. The greatest light comes looking for us. This is the season to smile in remembrance.

12

The Manger Display

We were given a manger display from my wife's grandparents. And we make sure to set it up in a prominent place each year. There's something sacred about so many hands touching the same objects over the years, as if touch could mark time. I like thinking that the ninety-three-year-old fingers of my wife's grandmother held the same baby Jesus that I hold, that our children hold. Every year, he's placed at the center of the grass-thatched manger, surrounded by shepherds, lambs, and wise men—and his two doting parents, of course. Sometimes our youngest, who loves babies, carries Jesus around to play with him all day, and I smile at the irony that our whole family has to go looking for baby Jesus at some point, under the couch cushions, under the table, somewhere in the playroom. Where is Jesus?

It's not a ridiculous question, really. We ask the same one of the real Jesus, deep in the caverns of our hearts. *Where is Jesus?* "Ascended at the right hand of the Father, making intercession for you"—I know, I know. I'm a theologian by training. But there's spiritual mystery for us, too. Jesus is a *person*, and he's with us in a different way than every other person who has walked into the dusty path of our lives. Though he's always with us (Matt. 28:20), there's a sense in which we always go looking for him, under the couch cushions of our experience, under the table of our thoughts, somewhere in the playroom of each day. Where is Jesus?

Setting up the manger each year, putting that thumb-sized baby in his little trough, orchestrating all the other characters around *him*—these things help us remember: Jesus is at the center. We swirl through the chaos of the day, caught up in whirlwinds of thought and worry. Jesus is at the center. We lose patience and huff at the slowness of others. Jesus is at the center. We fall short of expectations and are slow of heart to believe the smallest promise of God. Jesus is at the center. We shudder at words like "cancer" and "Alzheimer's." Jesus is at the center. Whether we realize it or not, Jesus is *always* at the center. "From him and through him and to him are all things" (Rom. 11:36). Jesus is the centering sun of our little universes.

Just as with the sun, we're mostly unaware of him. But that doesn't mean he's not constantly pulling us around himself with the unseen gravity of grace. He's giving us identity, possibility, and purpose at every second—*from* him, *through* him, *to* him. Jesus, our centering sun.

We need reminders. That's where the manger comes in. The camels and the wise men (and that one sheep with the bent leg) usually fall over. And every neat and ordered arrangement comes to chaos eventually. Little hands want to move the pieces. And we *want* our kids to touch the display, to grip the characters in their little fingers, to have a favorite. But baby Jesus always ends up back at the center, the object of every character's gaze.

Thank God for the mangers he gives us, the calls to keep setting Jesus at the center. No matter what happens amidst the rush and bustle of the season, we can keep putting Jesus where he belongs, at the center. In the deepest sense, he's always there, calling everything else to circle around him—livestock, wise men, shepherds, family . . . *us*.

13

The Frost in the Grass

ovember has crept up on us like a shoe-less child, scattering his silver dust in the night. We wake each morning to find the grass covered in tiny ice crystals, which catch the sun's first light at dawn and turn it into diamonds. In a few hours, as the sun settles on it, the frost will disappear. Like so much of God's living art, it's ephemeral, stitched into time just long enough for someone to notice (or not) before the stitch comes out. It *wasn't*, then it *is*, and then it's *not*. That's the meter in every line of life. The question has always been what we're supposed to do in the middle of the line.

The line of Christmas this year will follow the same meter. Right now we're in *wasn't*, while every child begs for *is*. It's a wonderful place to be. The anticipation for something holy and good, something engraved with an ancient joy—that's the best kind of anticipation. It feels like some call of God from above, as if his voice were floating to us from the future like a red-tailed hawk on a thermal. My God, how we stare at the future!

It will pass so very quickly, like that frost on our front lawn. We'll stand in the sun of this Christmas, and in a matter of moments, we'll look around us and realize the frost has melted. Time has taken back what it gave.

But the beauty of Christmas lies precisely in this: time has never been able to really take it away. Sure, the season passes each year before we know it, but Christmas is the coming. Christmas is the great tale of arrival: the God of mountains, music, and mercy came *here*. And the coming can never be undone.

The arrival of Jesus Christ is not like the frost on the morning grass. It appears to be, but look more closely. Life's meter of *wasn't*, *is*, and *is not* tells us that everything is passing away, and therefore we can't really possess anything. Our fleeting moments are lost on us. But for those of us who embrace Christ, we *can* possess something precious. In fact—and read these words slowly—*we possess everything* because he came. The Apostle Paul says this twice (1 Cor. 3:21; 2 Cor. 6:10). How can we possibly possess everything? Because we possess the person of Christ. Christmas is about God coming so that we could have him, not in some selfish sense, but in the sense God intended all along: we possess Christ so that we can give him.

Having everything means we don't have to chase after anything. We can look at every morning frost with pleasure instead of pain. It's not that we're losing things as time passes. We already possess all things because we possess the person from whom, through, and to whom they're all going (Rom. 11:36). And when your heart believes this, you can watch the world changing and marvel.

The frost may disappear in the morning sun, but the God who made that frost, who painted billions of blades of grass in white diamonds just for a few passing hours . . . that God lives in your chest. And it's all because he *came*. Christmas is about waking up and realizing your riches can't even be counted. And so you can go and give, worshiping with open hands.

14

The Slow-Rising Sun

I am always up before dawn. It's been a practice for many years now. I get up in the dark, have some black coffee, read my Bible, pray, and then write until the sun comes up. That means I can usually see the slow progress of the sunrise. It's too slow to see the motion of the sun lifting itself over the horizon, but I pick my head up every few minutes to notice what color the light is as it bleeds through the trees.

There's usually a silent symphony of color giving itself to the countryside in soft movements. First the horizon blushes with embarrassment. The orange-red turns to pink as it brushes the underbellies of the clouds. Then there's a sort of adolescent orange, a burning gold that comes through as innocent pride, the sort a child has when no one's looking. The orange then gives way to gold. A purification has taken place; the richness has been purged. Yellow-gold stretches into the clouds, boasting of brightness. And then the colors of the yard take their familiar forms: the crazed chlorophyll grass—the hair of the earth; the broken red wheel-barrow sleeping in the overgrown weeds; the yellow maple leaves, nearly finished their conversation with the November cold. The day is here.

The slowness of the sunrise is something I wish I could slow even more. I want to stretch it out for a few more hours so I can live a bit longer in each color. Those reds and oranges and golds deserve a longer stay.

I wonder sometimes what the sunrise was like the morning after Jesus's birth. Was it gray and cloudy silver because the world was dazed by the arrival of God? Was it gold like the streets of paradise? What colors struck the skin of Joseph and Mary as they walked in the world that housed

God incarnate?

We'll never know, at least not until we see Jesus face to face and ask him (I'll try to remember for us). But in a deeper sense, that little infant was already the start of the sunrise. He is, after all, the *light* (John 8:12). This was *his* dawn. He was on the cusp, on the world's edge, running headlong over the sleeping trees and drooping grass; finding every rooftop, every window frame, every wall, caressing an entire planet and sundry civilizations with the potent but soothing presence of his Lordship.

Christmas is the sunrise. Christ, you are *my* sunrise. You dawned when I was still in a daze from the dark. You came quiet and slow, filling my horizon with colors of hope, taking over the whole sky. It's in you that I lift my sleeping head and find the light ready and waiting. Jesus, my sunrise. Keep me mindful that Christmas is the day of divine dawn.

15

Golden Geese

So many moments of deep beauty in life seem to jump out and grab your hand when you aren't paying attention. That's why we'll always need children. They aren't afraid to clutch your fingers and pull you into the moment. That is what happened with the golden geese yesterday afternoon. I can't believe I almost missed it.

The sun had already fallen behind the trees. The day was in its humble retreat. A layer of transparent gold was rolling itself over the blue sky. The girls were dancing on the front walkway to Christmas music. And then they stopped as their heads shot upwards. "Dad, look: geese!" Nora wouldn't stop at that. "Look! Over there! They look gold."

We all looked up as the flock in V formation passed over our house, maybe forty feet above us. Nora was right. The setting sun, which we thought was nearly gone, had painted the underbellies of the geese with gold. As they flapped their wings in unison, the gold light shimmered. Their voices broke through the quiet, cackling in joy about the heat that lay in store for them. What might it be like to fly as a family, as a tribe, up above the tree line?

Those golden geese etched themselves on the stone of my memory. They were heading south, as they do each year. They were making a journey toward heat, leaving the cold behind their feet . . . flapping gold fleeing the cold. We wouldn't see their arrival, only their exit.

The same could be said of every human soul. "We won't see their arrival, only their exit." That doesn't have to be melancholy. We stood in the grass marveling at the golden geese as they flapped away from us. We were happy for their future arrival. We were also happy to watch their present exit.

I think about death often because, as a teenager, I watched my father die. The experience shattered me. I was *not* happy to watch his exit, though I believed in his arrival with God, his unseen migration to the land of life. Christmas, for me, is a time for the Spirit to rejuvenate that belief. It's a time for golden geese to overtake the memories of white hospital sheets and the smell of astringents. It's a time to remember that, in Christ, beginnings replace endings, light replaces darkness, migration replaces melancholy.

Christmas is for the golden geese and for those of us who stare into the sky, happy just to have seen the travel. What grounds do we have for such happiness? Just these: that on a night when no one suspected anything of happening, the gold light of eternity took on arms, legs, and skin. He came to lead our migration, to be the point of our flying V, taking us into the country of God, where geese are always gold and hope is always green.

16

The Presents Come Wrapped

Present wrapping has never been a strong suit for me. I have my moments of clean lines and tight corners, but they're far and few between. I do my best to cover what's inside, and I tell myself that's the important thing. Conceal what's on the inside . . . but not so well that a three-year-old can't tear through the paper and tape. This is a fascinating ritual we've developed, and it reveals a great deal about the Christmas story.

Why do we wrap gifts? It's not a trick question. We don't want people to see what's on the inside, right? Except, we do. We just don't want them to see it *yet*. *Yet* is the heart of present wrapping. "Can I see it?" The wrapping paper says in silence, "Not yet, but soon." The *yet* is what tantalizes children all over the world right about now. But if the *yet* were gone, they would be so disappointed. The *yet* makes them cringe, but it also makes them smile. It's the anticipation—a stirring of mystery in joy, like cream in coffee.

Was it all that different on the first Christmas morning? In one sense, it was because there were few who were truly anticipating the coming of the messiah. Some were looking for him, such as Simeon (Luke 2:25–26). But most weren't. They had no idea that the greatest gift God could give was on its way.

In another sense, the coming of Christ was very much like our wrapped gifts today, but infinitely more profound. God, all Israelites knew, could never show himself without some sort of mediation on this side of paradise. It was common knowledge that anyone who would see God's face without a mediator, without wrapping, would die (Exod. 33:20). It would be too much for them, like staring at the sun from a mile away. They'd be obliterated by holy light that would scream through human eyes in an instant. And yet God promised to come, to walk among his people. How would this happen? Through wrapping.

"And the Word became flesh and dwelt among us, and we have seen his glory, glory as of the only Son from the Father, full of grace and truth" (John 1:14). Could we paraphrase it? "And God wrapped himself as a present for us to hold, and we have held him and seen his beauty, beauty as of the only Son of the Father, full of giving." God wrapped and gave *himself* as the first Christmas gift.

Now, if we hold that gift and then dare to unwrap it, we will see the Father (John 14:9) in the power of the Holy Spirit. God only gives trinitarian gifts. But this gift does not have one day of the year for us to anticipate. It's a gift we wake up holding each day. We have a thousand opportunities every week to open the gift, to open God (the Son) *from* God (the Father) *by* God (the Spirit). It's always Christmas, in a sense.

But how do we know we've opened the gift?

The gift itself said it is more blessed to *give* than to receive (Acts 20:35). We know we've opened the grand Christmas gift (the gift of God for us) if we turn to someone else with open hands, if we give something of ourselves to others. Giving begets giving.

The *yet* of God's grand Christmas gift is still alive and well. The anticipation is ours, every waking minute. Christmas is simply a time to remember in song and gratitude what God is offering incessantly: the gift of himself that came wrapped and ready for us on a cold dark night two thousand years ago.

17

When the Tree Goes Up

Evergreens have long been a symbol of enduring life. The towering white pine trees guarding our property are shedding amber needles now, emptied of chlorophyll at the end of their life cycle. But the trees keep most of their needles through the winter. Their life outlasts the cold. They keep going when their deciduous brothers bow out, dropping their leaves and standing bare and gray against the clouds. Evergreens endure.

Some early pagan religions practiced hanging evergreens in their homes to promote the same life inside their walls that they found outside.

Egyptians even did this to declare the victory of life over death. This was a precursor to our modern Christmas tree tradition. But it was 16th century Germans who first brought whole trees inside their homes. And by the time it reached America in the 19th century, it was seen by many as a threatening distraction to what Christmas was really about (Christ)—not to mention that it was just plain odd. Why lift a living thing out of the earth and drag into your living room? We've lost that sense of oddity. But it doesn't take much to get it back. Take anything else from outside and put it on your kitchen table. Does it look as if it belongs? Dirt, roots, and limbs feel more at home in the soil than in a study or family room.

Still, there's something here for us. The ancient pagans thought evergreens symbolized life over death, especially because agriculture was literally their livelihood. They could never fathom that life would actually defeat death in a *person*, that a man would come back from the dead, that the greenery of life wouldn't just outlast the winter; it would leave the land of the living entirely, every season and sound, but then come back to breathe again. Christ is greater than evergreen; he's death-defeating. He didn't hold death off for a bitter season; he went through it. Down through the dark and dread he flew, returning to the light in three days. Evergreens stay when it's cold. But Christ left and came back. That's what the author of life does.

And still, we have our Christmas trees in the house, pieces of the world we've taken in for decoration. God, may we do that with Christ every morning. Although, as we struggle to focus in carrying something into our hearts, we'll always be surprised that he was already there. We didn't need to go and fetch him. What we were carrying was something else . . . an idea maybe. The *person* of Christ is always in our living room, tree or no tree. Better than an evergreen, he's life-giving, not just life-sustaining.

We can always put up the tree, but life has already been hung on a tree for us. And when they took his body down, that was *not* the end.

18

The Ember Glows

---◆---

We grew up in a house with a wood stove, out in the Pennsylvania country, below the Pocono mountains. Having a fire going from October to March was part of the routine of life. So many textures and smells are branded into my soul from those years: the fibrous strings peeling off split oak and maple; the touch of soft, wet bark left sleeping on the leaves for weeks; the sweet, inviting scent of smoke as it trickled out the top of the chimney and vanished like a thread of thought.

My favorite age for a fire is several hours,

just after the logs have mostly burned up and all that remain are glowing embers. It's the remnant of what began, the wood that stayed through the heat—reduced, heaving light in soft pulses. I could stare at embers for hours. Their glow doesn't shout, like the glow of many other lights; the ember glow whispers, giving off heat without calling attention to itself. In the world of light, embers are the humble servants every flame relies on to flicker and dance. And I feel at home among them.

The humble ember glow reminds me of the Spirit, who never calls attention to himself. He burns long and slow in the souls of those who embrace Jesus Christ. The Spirit is the heartwood of God, the one who knows the thoughts of the Father in the fullness of the Son (1 Cor. 2:10–11). And the heartwood Spirit was with Christ even in the womb, for Mary was found to be with child "from the Holy Spirit" (Matt. 1:18).

There, in the uterus of a woman, wrapped and waiting, lay the Son of God, with the Spirit burning long and slow like an ember. Nine months of a long, slow burn.

But the baby Christ of Christmas was not a

fading fire. With the Spirit ever beneath him, he was a growing flame, building in power and light by the Spirit's presence. And when he emerged from his mother on that Bethlehem night, a white flame broke into the world. In the spiritual realm, it must have seemed as if a star had tumbled out of a woman. So much light. Such brightness, hugged by a world of dark, absorbing whatever it could of him.

The Spirit rested in Christ as he grew in wisdom and stature (Luke 2:52). As the ember beneath the flame of his incarnate life, the Spirit burned long and slow as Jesus walked and touched and tasted and slept.

Jesus, when the world thought you went out, you glowed back from the dead, still and strong and silent . . . like an ember nodding to the air of doubt, unthreatened, unflinching.

Jesus, my humble Lord, ever burning above the ember of the Spirit, light my way this Christmas with your amber glow. Draw me in closer so I can feel the heat and put out my hands to receive it.

19

A Holy Night

The most beautiful song I've ever heard is "O Holy Night." It's a deep and mysterious anthem for a deep and mysterious evening. It's hard to describe how the melody meets my soul, but it's something like a lantern meeting a winter evening in the snow, the gold light greeting the navy night and bowing before broad silhouettes within its radius. The song always drives a rivet into my chest, wherever I am. It makes me say, "Yes . . . the night *was* holy."

Perhaps my favorite line is, "Till he appeared and the soul felt its worth." How does a soul *feel* its worth? I don't know. But . . . maybe I do. There are some moments when we recognize ourselves in a way that both meets and transcends the ordinary. We see clearly *who* and *where* we are in the grand scheme of God's wild providence—an open field calls our eyes into a green expanse and the unsearchable riches of nature; a Third Eye Blind song makes us think of that boy who took his life in the ninth grade; a cancer-ridden pastor who tells us from the pulpit that all we really want is to see the face of God, and we believe him. We each have our own examples. We feel our soul's worth whenever we see ourselves orbiting something much greater, as if Mars were to wake up content with his path, even grateful for it, realizing with awe that the sun *should* be getting all the attention (just look at it!). When we know that we're deeply valued and loved and yet not central to everyone else's existence, *that's* when the soul feels its worth.

But the *appearing* of Christ—that's what triggers our realization. That previous line—"Long lay the world in sin and error pining"—is where you and me slept. The whole world was sleeping, laying in a dark bed, yearning for something greater, something beyond itself. We had, in a deep sense, forgotten our worth. It's a worth God gives, not a worth we earn. God made us like himself; that's where we find our worth, in mirroring him. And we remembered this with horror, remorse, and joy when Christ appeared. That's when our souls feel their worth, when they see who we could and should be in the wondrous Word of God, when we orbit happily as planets around the center star of God.

And then comes that glorious call to fall on our knees and hear the angel voices, those voices that dropped the jaws of sleepy shepherds, those voices steeped in the abiding presence of God.

Oh, that night is holy. It was the night God spoke himself into our world, as we lay sleeping in self-centered doubt and spiritual pneumonia, our lungs too weak to take in the full truth. The night that Christ appeared was the night we found our breath and rose, only to fall back down on our knees in worship.

Maybe that's what Christmas is really about: God in Christ rousing us from our sleep so that we can feel our soul's worth only to fall back down and sing about it. We wake. We rise. We feel. We fall. The whole thing ends in worship, where it should have begun. We have our chance again, right now. A holy night beckons us to stare at Christ, feel our worth in him, and lift our hands up to the navy sky.

20

Sledding

———◆———

We grew up in a house at the top of a hill. The ditch ran all the way down to the bottom, but then it broke off to the left, going even farther down below the road, to a little pond. That made the ultimate sledding track. Once the track had been packed down by a few runs, little fist holes marking the sides of the sled impression, it was ready. Ready for what? Ready for us to build up jumps, of course. We got some serious air beneath those wild-colored Walmart sleds each year. We also broke several of them, which made us pretty proud. Not every kid can tell stories about the sledding track that ends in broken shards of plastic.

Our golden retrievers (we always had at least one) would get so excited when we started at the top. They'd try to bite our snowsuit sleeves and pull us down the hill, before they realized we were going faster than they were. My God, I still remember Hunter's brown-gold coat waving amidst the snowfall as some wild energy worked itself out in galloping paws and street-scraping glove marks.

Everyone loves to glide. Sledding reminds you of that. For me, the ease was always more important than the speed—just to be able to drift and feel the soft bumps of snow beneath your knees. That's what made the long trek back up the hill worth it.

It was a lot of work to build the track. Sometimes, if the snow was deep, we had to push ourselves down the whole hill, pressing our weight into the sled to pack the snow. But each time one of us went down the track, it tightened, solidified, became a true path through the white. The repetition led to the ease of the ride. The more we went down, the smoother the track became. After several runs, we all could enjoy the ease, racing down the track without having to push our weight forward. We could truly *ride* the sled.

I suppose you could say the prophets did that for Christ. They kept pushing themselves down the track of God's coming, making a way. "In the wilderness prepare the way of the LORD; make straight in the desert a highway for our God" (Isa. 40:3). The desert is the opposite of Pennsylvania snow, of course. But the idea is there. John the Baptist was the last one to smooth out the sledding track for Christ (Mark 1:1–4). And the first Christmas night was when Christ arrived at the top of the hill, gazing down the track of his life by starlight, the track of God's coming.

The track, however, would not be easy coasting for Christ. The way was clear for him, but he had to fight every step against forces of evil that wanted him to turn aside, to give up, to take another way (Matt. 4:1–11). Our faithful savior went all the way down, even into the pits of hell.

And he came back. His resurrection is what solidified the track for *us*. Now we follow Christ down the track of God's coming. We have the ease he lacked; we know what lies ahead—life and hope and peace—and so we can ride with confidence and clarity. God, how much of life is following Christ's back down the slope of life, clinging to the end of his sled? *All of it.*

Any ease we have in living is because of the impressions Christ has made. And the ride began on Christmas, on the night that God's coming finally became a *person*, Immanuel.

When I see Christ in glory, I'm going to ask him if we can go sledding together. I suspect he would smile and say, "We already did."

21

The Smell of Snow

***

Right before it snows, there's a scent in the air. And I've always loved it. I read recently that there's not really a particular scent; it's more like a sensation in your nose. The cold temperature brings the humidity down, which dries up your nose and deadens your sense of smell. At the same time, the change in temperature and humidity can also activate a special nerve in your nose that picks up on things such as the cooling sensation of mint. All these details combine, really, to help us pick up on a *change*. Something is about to happen. What *wasn't* will soon become what *is*, and you're sitting on the cusp of it. There's a thrill in that. That thrill is a beautiful parallel of what happens inside me as Christmas draws near. Change is coming.

"No, that's not quite right," some people would say. "The change already happened. Christmas is just when we remember the change." That's true in a sense. The white-washing snowfall of grace in Christ happened only once and for all. At Christmas, we remember the birth of grace incarnate.

But in another sense, change comes every year (even every second), for Christ is a *person*, not an event. We experience him in ongoing, ever-deepening relationship. Christmas season is a special time for that relationship. It's a remembrance of grace given, but it's also an experience of the person of grace, moment by moment. People speak of "receiving Christ" as if he were a fancy table runner. We open the package, lay it out before us, and rejoice. And then it gets stored away with the napkins and table cloths. *That is not what we do with a person.* A person is lived with; a person is experienced fresh each day. A person listens and speaks.

And so I wait with bated breath on the cusp of change—every day, but also with special enthusiasm as Christmas approaches. The anticipation of renewal, of recognizable change in spirit, of even a rebirth of hope and faith—these are the things that bring a childhood smile back to my aging face. Christmas is coming. Change is imminent, like the snow on freezing winter nights, when all the conditions are . . . perfect.

Coming snow smells like change. Whenever I notice it, I pause and take in a deep breath of the cold air. I gather the potential, the dream of whiteness, the joy of soft feathers falling from the dark sky. I pull it all in through my nostrils and hold it inside my chest for a few seconds. Then I let it out slowly. Change is coming.

Christmas is a season in which we open ourselves to change, to the change ushered in by the most beautiful person the world has ever known. The conditions are perfect. Everything is in its right place. Jesus, be my snowfall. Fall down from everywhere. Surround me. Cover the face of the earth.

22

The Silence of Night

W hen you grow up in the Pennsylvanian countryside, the evenings bring a chorus of crickets and cicadas. Night is never silent in the spring or summer. Even into the fall, before the first frost, the insects are singing into the black, holding nothing back. But after that first frost, as old man winter dusts the leaves from the trees and calls in the barrenness of ice, the silence enters. And it's very strange at first, as if a great arena had emptied of all spectators, and you're standing in the center wondering when they'll come back. But the silence grows on you as the season soldiers on. It becomes peaceful. It's a time of rest. The silence of night is the solace of stillness.

Tonight I smelled the smoke from our chimney as I walked down the driveway; pink wisps of cloud faded into the deep purple of evening, like drifting memories. All was quiet. The crickets and the bees and the tiny toads are gone. They've left. Winter's joints have already cracked as he laid himself down across the atmosphere. He's here now, covering everything. I stand still in the driveway for a moment. I breath in the air and stare into the surrounding trees. I love this quiet.

It's temporary, I know. The silent night is beautiful but brief. All these winter silences will turn to spring songs soon enough. But I enjoy while I'm here. This present is *my* present. The quiet brings focus, and the cold air brings clarity.

I like to think of that silent night of Christ's birth. There were voices, sure. And the grunts and huffs of cattle, the rustling of hooves in the hay. There were sounds, but a surrounding silence. From *this* woman would come not merely sound, but a Son. Into the silent night would come Christ as king.

As the darkness is an arena for the light, the silence would be an arena for his sounds— the fragile humming and cooing, the brittle cries for embrace. Like the rest of us, Christ had been wrapped in a warm embrace for nine months. It's hard to go without a hug every few seconds when that's been your steadfast environment.

It's hard not to take the silence and marry it to John 1:1. The hymn says, "Silent night, holy night." It was silent and holy because the very speech of God was being pushed into the open. Divine utterance was given a human audience. *This* is God, the one who speaks with star-setting, mountain-raising, water-wielding authority. Into the silence came *this* sound. And it would be a sound to cause the rise and fall of many souls (Luke 2:34).

While it's true that silence brings the solace of stillness, it's also true that the sound of Christ brings the peace of paradise. He brought eternity here, carried it with him into that silent night. While the whole world kept spinning, raucous and discontent, he came into a little patch of silence, a sound to save all things.

23

What's Your Gift?

Gold, frankincense, and myrrh. Those are the famous gifts brought to baby Jesus. We often focus on the gifts themselves rather than the *act of giving*. Try to make yourself unfamiliar with the Christmas story. Three magi, three human beings, made a great journey across the earth—on camel backs, over dunes, and through deserts—chasing after a star that would point down to a birthplace for a stranger. How would they meet this stranger whom they believed would be a great king? They would bring *gifts*, expressions of value and adoration. They carried concrete manifestations of their hearts for an infant king.

I don't know why I'd never thought of this before: why do I bring nothing with me when I celebrate his birth? I've walked into dozens of Christmas Eve services empty handed. Haven't you? We carry nothing with us.

It's different for us, of course, than it was for the magi. But the spirit of that first Christmas act, the first gift giving, is still with us. When we go to celebrate the birth of Christ, it would make perfect sense to carry something with us, something that would express our heart's disposition toward him. It wouldn't be gold or some strange spice. But it could be something . . . *precious*.

God loves words; he's their origin. Maybe that would be a fitting gift for the king of speech: one, wholesome, memory-steeped word. There's no shortage of them, and they don't take up any pocket space. You could carry it with you in silence, as the magi carried their gifts through the dark of night and haze of day, letting the gifts rest in their baggage. All the while, God could see. He sees everything, all that's hidden under leather and cloth, all that's tucked quietly behind the walls of a mind. He sees. And he smiles.

What will you choose? I think I have mine for this year: *blanket*. It's a rich word, full of history and scented with a thousand experiences. The water is a blanket for the ocean bottom, the air a blanket for the earth. We make our blankets by drawing together tiny threads, unifying the particulars of cotton or wool or nylon, gathering what is separate, making it one. I think God loves that idea.

And then there are blankets for bodies. God's own Son was wrapped in cloth that would also be used for his burial. That's not a morbid thought; it's beautiful. Bodies come into the world with coverings, and they go out in coverings, too. After birth, the covering conceals, locking in the heat that radiates from blood flow. In burial, the cloth protects our hands from the coldness of death. But it also wraps the body like a present, keeping it ready for a Christmas resurrection, somewhere on the horizon of the future.

Yes, *blanket*. That will be the gift I bring for baby Jesus this year. It isn't much, but neither is gold to the maker of mountains. Words are precious to the Word. In my heart, I know he will unwrap it with joy, and in love for the giver. That's my gift this year, the concrete manifestation of my heart, a fitting present for the one who wraps my soul in the new cloth of himself (Rom. 13:14). Jesus . . . my blanket.

What's your gift?

24

White as Snow

Do you remember the words of Isaiah, words from the mouth of God? "Come now, let us reason together, says the LORD: though your sins are like scarlet, they shall be as white as snow" (Isa. 1:18). From scarlet to snow . . . quite the transformation. How could one become the other? How can the red of rebellion be washed by the white of holy ice? The answer God gives is beautifully mysterious: *through a person given*. The change of colors is the work of Christ.

I don't think about this at Christmas. I'm not sure why. Maybe I'm caught up in all the songs that talk about the joy of God's coming, the wonder of arrival, the heralding of hope. Those things are all appropriate. But in the end, I think more about the entrance of God and less about the colors of my soul. But the coming of God would bring no comfort to a scarlet soul. It would only bring comfort if snow was promised.

But . . . it *is*. That's what Isaiah writes. God promises to change our colors, from war-waging red to winter white. It's in his coming, the coming of Christ, that God takes out a new palette of paint. Wetting his brush with words, he soaks his bristles in that winter white, and he starts waving over our reds. Gone are the lies and lusts, the dread and the doubt, the heavy fetters of unholy desires. Every whisper of want and thought of ill intent is covered over. All is white. All is white.

Christmas is our color change. A little infant makes his way out of a woman's body, and God has arrived. In the world of spirits, snow has begun to fall with his first breath. Christ brings the snow of grace. It's covering all the red souls meandering through the markets or cruising down the highway, asleep in their beds or running along the roadways.

All the red souls are turning white.

When it comes to the soul, God does with the weather what we could never do in our dreams. The snow of grace comes down with Christ, like manna from heaven. "What *is* this?" The Israelites asked the same question in the wilderness. "It's grace . . . just grace, enough to change your colors."

25

Missing Christmas

There were only a select few who witnessed the birth of Christ, and most of them were probably animals. Aside from Joseph, Mary, some shepherds, and the magi, most people missed Christmas in that sense. But that didn't matter, since Christmas could still be *received* by them even after it happened. That's what we do today. But there was at least one person who truly missed Christmas. His name was Herod.

In chasing after Christ to put an end to his new life, King Herod slaughtered all the male children in Bethlehem who were two years old or younger. It was a horror beyond words. These little boys . . . newly lit candles, just beginning to burn in the world, were snuffed out by a narcissistic tyrant. And his effort was futile anyway. Baby Jesus fled in his mother's arms to Egypt before the sword and spear could reach his hometown. Herod's act was reckless and desperate. He brought searing pain to innocent mothers and fathers just for the *chance* to protect his throne.

Herod missed Christmas because he missed Christ. But he *really* missed him. That baby was divine love incarnate, and Herod wanted to kill him. Why? Because he was so focused on his own self-preservation that he couldn't see the selfless love of God. And trying to wipe out that selfless love of God was an attempt at wiping out redemption for every man, woman, and child who has ever lived. Herod missed Christmas, alright. But he was almost foolish enough to make the whole world miss it, too.

Of course, Herod never stood a chance. God's providence is perfect. Herod could never lay hand on Christ, let alone the blade of a sword. Christmas was coming whether Herod wanted it or not. He could either embrace it and bow in submission to the glory of God or tear the world apart like a toddler in rage. He chose the latter. And he caused such pain to parents who were just beginning to enjoy their sons. Many of those little boys hadn't started walking all that long ago. They were still finding their feet. And the rage of a black-hearted madman stole them away. I can't think of it for too long without being filled with anger.

But, you know, we can be like Herod, too. In a horrid and terrorizing way, Herod was merely placing *himself* above God. The Lord of the universe was coming. Herod tried to say "no." He wanted to remain the center of his pathetic little world. He wanted everyone to be secondary to his own rule, even the Son of God. In our quieter ways, we do the same thing every year, don't we? We act as if Christmas is primarily about us in some sense— the gifts we give or receive, the places we go, the people we see. In subtle ways, we place ourselves above God. We spend our minutes thinking not about the coming of God in flesh but the coming of a day in the month. Christ fades out of our Christmas.

Herod may have been the one who truly missed Christmas, but that doesn't keep us from missing Christmas each year, from somehow making it about ourselves. The key to *not* missing it, to grabbing onto Christmas with white-knuckled joy, is to travel . . . like the shepherds, like the magi. We have to travel to the manger. We have to travel to the place where the whole world was on the edge of a precipice. And there, in a humble, ordinary space filled with ordinary people, we have to thank God for the arrival—the pure, holy thrill of God's arrival.

If we can do that, we won't have missed Christmas. If we can do that, Christmas will have found *us*.

26

The Face of God

———◆———

What did their faces look like when they saw him? Mary. Joseph. The shepherds. The magi. What did their faces look like? Was it just curiosity, or awe—raised eyebrows and open jaws? Or was it a deeper, quiet hope relaxing their brow and cheek muscles? Maybe I'll ask them one day. These questions kneel in submission, however, to the question of what *his* face was like.

A beloved pastor and friend was once preaching what would end up being one of his final sermons. He had been battling stomach cancer for years, and things had taken a darker turn unexpectedly. I only remember one moment from this sermon, and I don't think it will ever leave me. "Isn't this what you want more than anything: to see the face of God?"

God is a Spirit (John 4:24). We go all our lives praying to a three-personed God whom we're told is more personal than any other being, who *created* personhood itself. Yet, we've never seen his face. And a face is a portrait of a person, where the colors and lines and eyes—my God, the eyes!—reveal identity in an instant. To see the face of God, this most personal hearth of love and life and hope . . . yes, that's what I want more than anything else. I want to see God's face. At the end of my life, be it tomorrow or fifty years from now, I hope to close my eyes and then open them to gaze at the broad, strong, smiling face of God.

At the manger, however, there was a priceless opportunity to see the face of the Son of God incarnate. Jesus's face was the one chosen by the Lord of the universe. His nose, his eyes, his cheeks and chin—these were all selected by God himself. This was not *the* face of God in an ultimate sense, but it certainly was *a* face of God. And only a small group in human history got to see it.

But just the fact that God would do this, that he would give himself a human face, renders me speechless. It's as if, after thousands of years, God said, "Now it's time. I'll give myself a face they can see and touch, just for a little while."

Now *that* is the ultimate Christmas gift. In Jesus, God gave us what we most long for—to see the face of God. I know what you're thinking. "Well, that's great for those select few in history, but *I* never got to see him. None of us knows what Jesus looks like. Why can't *we* see his face?" I can't answer that question. What I can say in response, though, is that if God was willing to wrap himself in flesh, to give himself a skeleton and optic nerves and fingerprints, all so we could see that he *really* loves us that much, enough to pull back the cloudy curtain of time and step onto the stage for just a moment, then I'm happy. My faith is in that. He came! He gave himself a face for us, a promise that his great face will one day meet ours, and we won't even be able to fathom it. Moses got to see God's great back (Exod. 33:18–20), but we'll all get to gaze into God's glorious face. I imagine it will be more expansive than the sky itself. It will take us in, staring at us until we're fully seen and known (1 Cor. 13:12).

Christmas is the coming of God's face. That's cause for a million hallelujahs. I'll sing out the same when I see the great face of God one day.

27

The Messenger

G od loves to send messengers. Of all the hosts of heavenly angels, there was *one* God called forward to deliver the message (Luke 2:8–14). From the unseen canopy of paradise came this one angel, trailed by a multitude of light-gilded kin. The audience? No kingly court or gathering of religious elites; just a pack of grass-grazing shepherds, trying to sleep in shifts through the night.

We think of the awe those shepherds felt. But what of that one messenger? What of the news-carrier? I like to slow things down. Before the angel came, was there a meeting? Or did the Father, Son, and Spirit simply call his name and nod. "Now is the time. Go on. And take your kin with you." What would the angel say? "My Lord, how many of them shall I bring?" A simple response: "All of them. Fill up the night sky."

And then he came down. Sure. Silent. He found the shepherds exactly where they should be, in the perfect place to be dazed into worship. He delivered the message of good news and great joy: a *savior* was about to be born—not a king or a politician, but a *savior*. Did they know they needed one?

The angel's kin then began to glow, radiating, an army in the stars. They sang their native anthem of worship and then retreated into the navy night. The messenger's task was done.

But that was only the first messenger. The other messenger—the highest messenger—was wrapped in infant garments, nestled in a manger with his mother and father. People didn't even know that he was a messenger. He'd tell them later. "And the Father who sent me has himself borne witness about me" (John 5:37). This was the *divine* messenger. And the message he carried wasn't heralded from the sky; it was spoken plainly on the earth, among fishermen and tax collectors, among his parents and brothers, among the leaders who grew to hate him. His message was *himself*: God has come down to redeem.

That is a message even angels would marvel at. God as the messenger and the message? A *life* given as a word spoken? What if they didn't understand? What if they ignored him?

It was worse than that. They would jeer at him. They would crucify him. They would hang the message of God from a cross. And even when the message came back from the dead, they still wouldn't listen, deaf beyond deaf.

And yet still the message came on Christmas night, wrapped and weak, soft-boned and brittle, like a piece of paper in the wind. How could it last? How would people even hear him?

As with every message today, people hear it when they're *listening* for it. Anyone poor in spirit had open ears. They would hear. They would listen. And a building would start to rise, stone by stone. All because a messenger came, announcing God the *messenger*, God the *message*—and God, in the spirits of those who believed, also the *receiver*.

No one can keep God from speaking to his own. That's really what Christmas is about.

28

When the Sun Arrived

———◆———

It's really the day *after* Christmas that means the most to us, since we're still living in it. The glory and amazement of that night eventually settled with the still cattle hooves. Everything slept, even for a short time. And then the sun rose the next day. God had arrived. He had done what no one thought possible: entered the world in flesh. Now God was here. But what was the rest of the world to do? What are we to do now?

News changes the world. It changes our thoughts and behaviors. It alters our path. When what *wasn't* becomes what *is*, we choose to either align or adjust, to fall into the new path or create a different path that goes around the news. This is still the case for us with Christmas. God was born into the world—*God*. Slow down and think about that for a few moments. The Spirit who formed all things, including the majority of the universe that we haven't even seen yet, took on flesh. He showed up, when hope had been nearly forgotten. Now *that's* some news.

What did people do with it? What do we do with it? We either live *into* it or *around* it. To live into this news of God's coming is to surround ourselves with it, enclosing ourselves inside it as if we were traveling through some kind of spiritual capillary. All meaning, all rest, all motion, all joy lives *here*. God has come, and that changes everything.

To live *around* this news is to find something else to hold our attention: gifts, family, gatherings, travel, work. Whatever we can substitute for the grand gift of God, we do it. We steer ourselves around or above or beneath the cosmic good news of God's coming.

It's the day now. After that holy, silent night, the sun still rose. The next day came. All that remained was *the news*. That's what we still hold at this very second. We hold the news of God's coming. Every Christmas Eve service across the globe will talk about the "good news of great joy." But news that doesn't change us isn't really news; it's information, maybe even myth for some people. Even for many Christians, Christmas is more of an idea than an event; it comforts their conscience, but it doesn't change their path.

What would a change in our path look like? Very simple: *it would look like grace*. If the God of all things came to the earth to give his rebellious riffraff a million second chances, if he entered the Bethlehem countryside on a silent night, even as he was forming galaxies and controlling the explosions of stars, if that *really* happened, how could we possibly *not* live out of grace? How could we *not* search our days for second-chances we might give to others, encouragement that might lift them up, hope that might bolster their tired knees? If grace came down on Christmas night, how can we not show grace when the run rises on the day after?

Of all the things Christmas is, it must be grace, an unwarranted, unmerited visit from the

God who holds every leaf vein in place with the power of his word. Christmas is grace because Christ is grace.

The sun has risen now. The news is out. You have your choice. And I have mine. May this be the season you live *into* grace.

Other Books by the Author

You can connect with the author to learn more about his work, receive updates on forthcoming publications, and have regular correspondence with him. To do this, and to explore other books from the author, visit piercetaylorhibbs.com.

One of the ways in which you can bless an author is to leave the author a review on Amazon. Even a one-sentence review will help spread the message of hope in this book. Thank you for reading!

Made in United States
North Haven, CT
11 December 2021

12394524R00071